RELATIONSHIPS
RESOLVING CONFLICT AND BUILDING COMMUNITY

FOUNDATIONS FOR
CHRISTIAN LIVING
SERIES

NAVPRESS

BRINGING TRUTH TO LIFE
NavPress Publishing Group
P.O. Box 35001, Colorado Springs, Colorado 80935

The Navigators is an international Christian organization. Our mission is to reach, disciple, and equip people to know Christ and to make Him known through successive generations. We envision multitudes of diverse people in the United States and every other nation who have a passionate love for Christ, live a lifestyle of sharing Christ's love, and multiply spiritual laborers among those without Christ.

NavPress is the publishing ministry of The Navigators. NavPress publications help believers learn biblical truth and apply what they learn to their lives and ministries. Our mission is to stimulate spiritual formation among our readers.

Cover Photo by Bruce Ayres / Tony Stone Images

The FOUNDATIONS FOR CHRISTIAN LIVING (FCL) series grew out of The Navigators' worldwide Scriptural Roots of the Ministry (SRM) process. The eight guides in this series reflect the major themes that emerged from ten years of Scriptural study, international dialogue, and prayer. It is the desire of the SRM team that those who follow Jesus Christ be grounded in these fundamental elements of the faith. For more information regarding the SRM process, please write to NavPress at the above address. The FCL series was researched and developed by Don Bartel, John Purvis, and Chuck Steen. The series text was written by Joanne Heim.

Unless otherwise identified, all Scripture quotations in this publication are taken from the HOLY BIBLE: NEW INTERNATIONAL VERSION ® (NIV®), Copyright © 1973, 1978, 1984 by International Bible Society, used by permission of Zondervan Publishing House, all rights reserved. The other versions used are The Message (MSG) by Eugene H. Peterson, © 1993, 1994, 1995, 1996, used by permission of NavPress Publishing Group; The Living Bible (TLB), © 1971, owned by assignment by the Illinois Regional Bank N.A. (as trustee), used by permission of Tyndale House Publishers, Inc., Wheaton, IL 60189; and the New Revised Standard Version (NRSV), © 1989, by the Division of Christian Education of the National Council of the Churches of Christ in the USA, used by permission, all rights reserved.

Printed in the United States of America

1 2 3 4 5 6 7 8 9 10 11 12 13 14 15 / 02 01 00 99 98 97

CONTENTS

HOW TO USE THIS GUIDE

For those God foreknew he also predestined to be
conformed to the likeness of his Son. . . .

—Romans 8:29

The French philosopher Jean-Paul Sartre quipped that "hell is other people." Unfortunately, sometimes that's just how it feels! Our relationships can bring us unmeasured joy but also pain and heartache.

When we experience difficulty in our relationships with people, we sometimes find ourselves having a harder time relating to God, too. It's been said that we have two kinds of relationships—vertical (our relationship with God) and horizontal (our relationships with others). What affects one easily affects the other.

The Bible has much to say about our relationships. In fact, it holds up the model of a caring community as the foundational benchmark of God's people. However, one look at Israel's history in the Old Testament or contemporary church practice reveals that this community we're meant to experience is easier described than achieved.

In this guide, we'll examine the nature of the community God intends for us to experience, and discover how to build healthy relationships that nurture us and draw others into the body of Christ.

The FOUNDATIONS Process

The FOUNDATIONS series will help you not merely learn about God but also grow in your love for Him. Through the FOUNDATIONS process you'll grow in discovering God, experiencing one another, and serving in the world. Your group will . . .

▶ pursue the mystery of God together and discover ways to draw closer to Him

▶ grow as you learn to be honest and vulnerable with one another, deeply accepting one another

► become courageous in helping one another at the point of personal need
► discover how to live genuinely in this fast-paced, complex world
► design ways to serve God together, as a group

The nine sessions in this study follow a three-stage process:

1. Session 1 introduces you to the FOUNDATIONS series. You'll explore three essential elements of the spiritual life on which the series focuses. You'll also begin to develop relationships with the other people in your small group. Session 1 is the same in all FOUNDATIONS studies. If you have recently used another FOUNDATIONS study with your current group, you may simply review session 1 of this study.
2. Sessions 2 through 7 lead you through a variety of issues related to resolving conflict and building community with others.
3. Sessions 8 and 9 enable you to take stock of what you've studied and consider what you want to do about it. In session 8 you'll discern how the material applies to you as an individual. Your group will offer feedback and support in following through. In session 9 you'll discuss how the material applies to you as a group. Most of the Bible was written to groups of people rather than to individuals, so session 9 may bring your study alive in ways you did not expect. Session 9 will also help you assess your group's progress in becoming a community as you look at unity, intimacy, interdependence, and mission.

A Modular Approach

Each session is divided into four modules or sections.

OVERVIEW

The overview section briefly describes where the session is headed and what your goals will be. The key issue is stated in the paragraph labeled "So, what's the big deal?" This issue will normally be a point of tension between what the Bible teaches and what we commonly experience. The session will then help your group wrestle through that tension together.

Stating the key issue up front risks preempting the Holy Spirit from guiding your group in the direction He wants to take it, but if you remain open to His leading throughout your individual preparation and group meeting, we believe He'll use the material to minister to you in ways you wouldn't have imagined.

ON YOUR OWN (30-60 minutes)

This section includes the passages you should be sure to examine before your group meets. You'll find some questions easy; others will stretch you mentally. We've found that a spiritual person is defined more by the internal questions he or she is asking than by the conclusions he or she has already reached. Mind-stretching questions are ideal for group discussion—be prepared for a lively debate! (And don't overlook the *For Further Study* questions, where we've hidden some of the best material in each session!)

As you work through this material, it will be helpful to remember a few "principles of understanding" that relate to learning about God:

► Understanding comes through mental exertion (Proverbs 2:3-5). Make sure you schedule enough preparation time to delve into the topic.

► Understanding comes through the soul and spirit (John 4:24). Seek God in your spirit as you study, as well as when you discuss.

► Understanding comes through the insight of others (Romans 1:12; Acts 17:11). Ask God to make you discerning so you will hear what He is saying to you through each other.

GROUP DISCOVERY (40-90 minutes)

This will be the discussion portion of your group meeting. It will usually include three sub-sections:

Let's Warm Up: Each group session opens with a question or two to help you learn about each other. The warm-up questions also help you move from what you were thinking about (or worried about) when you arrived at the meeting to what the biblical texts deal with. These questions put you in touch with the topic in an experiential way, so your discussion is not just sharing ideas but sharing life. The questions in this section always focus on life experiences and are usually fun to answer.

Let's Talk: In this section you'll examine one or two key Bible passages on the topic and discuss what light these passages shed on the central tension of the study. You'll also discuss any questions raised by your individual study. Feel free to bring to the group anything that perplexed or excited you in your individual study.

Let's Act: The questions in this section connect what you've studied to how you live. They often ask you to consider applying what you've learned to your group as a whole, rather than just to your individual life. Application is the reason for Bible study; be sure you allow plenty of time for it.

GROUP WORSHIP (15-30 minutes)

In order to stress the importance of the worship portion of your meeting, we have set it apart as a special section. Worship and prayer as a group are essential components of the FOUNDATIONS process. Praying and worshiping together can be one of the most faith-building and relationship-building activities you do together. Since many people have never prayed aloud with others before, the suggestions for worship begin gently. Later in the study you'll have an opportunity to plan your own worship times. You may decide to assign one person in the group to plan and lead worship, or you may rotate the responsibility.

In session 4 you'll begin to set aside at least 15 minutes of your worship time to discuss prayerfully and humbly a question often over-looked in Bible studies: "What is the Holy Spirit saying to us?" (This is referred to as *Let's Listen to God*.) You may find it challenging to get past what you imagine God ought to be saying to the group. The experience of trying to discern God's voice will invariably draw your group to a deeper level of intimacy.

Facilitator's Job Description

Leadership is essential to an effective group. FOUNDATIONS studies will go much better if someone in your group takes responsibility to:

1. Launch the group
   - ▶ Recruit people for the group, explaining its purpose and process.
   - ▶ Schedule meetings (with group consensus).

2. Pray regularly
   - ▶ For the individual members in their daily lives.
   - ▶ For the group's growth into community.
   - ▶ For the courage and faith of the group to take the steps it needs to grow in Christ.

3. Build community
   - ▶ Stay in touch with the members, encouraging them to also stay in touch with each other.
   - ▶ Make sure that each member grows in his or her ownership of this group. (This can be done by assigning responsibility—those with responsibility usually experience ownership and genuine membership in a group.)
   - ▶ Help the group move beyond studying to doing.
   - ▶ Maintain momentum and remotivate group members if enthusiasm diminishes.

4. Facilitate rather than lead
   - ▶ Search for vision and direction together, rather than announcing vision and answers. Help the group arrive at its vision and answers. Help people go where the Spirit is leading them, rather than where you think they should go. Remind them that understanding is only the beginning; implementing is the goal.
   - ▶ Teach by asking questions, rather than making authoritative statements. Questions can often accomplish what statements cannot. Questions were Jesus' preferred style.
   - ▶ Draw out the quiet or introverted persons.
   - ▶ Encourage everyone's participation; affirm the different contributions of all.

5. Be content with less than ideal progress
   ▶ Put up with some ambiguity. People never grow in a constant or straight line. Two steps forward and one step back is the norm. Remember what Christ has tolerated in you. Be happy with progress in the general direction of FOUNDATIONS goals.

6. Watch the clock
   ▶ When the allotted time for a given section is over, go on to the next section even if the group has not exhausted its discussion. (It is likely you will need to do this—many of the *Let's Talk* sections have more than enough material to fill the recommended time slot.) Unless you have unlimited time, the group will appreciate being kept on schedule. Don't allow discussion to consume all of your time so that application and worship must be omitted. On the other hand, if you sense the Spirit of God is actively at work, follow the Spirit's leading, not the clock. Look for an appropriate time at which to say, "I sense that God is doing something important here. Is it okay with all of you if we extend our time in this section of the meeting?"

7. Delegate
   ▶ After the first two or three sessions, ask someone else in the group to lead the worship time. Someone in your group is probably gifted in the area of worship and interested in helping the group focus on God through worship. Also, ask someone to lead the Group Discovery discussion. Direct that person to read item 4 in this job description. You could rotate this job around the group. Finally, appoint someone else to be timekeeper. By delegating these three functions, you will encourage all participants to feel like owners of the group rather than spectators.

8. Establish ground rules
   ▶ It is important that everyone in the group has a chance to buy into the rules by which the group will run. Ground rules clarify what the group expects from each person. The most important ground rules are stated on pages 17-18. Be sure to discuss them in your first meeting.

1.

THREE BIG IDEAS

In this introductory session you'll examine the three essential elements of the spiritual life on which the FOUNDATIONS series focuses: worship, community, and service. Your goals will be:

▶ To understand and own these three elements—worship, community, and service
▶ To get to know each other by telling a little of your stories and why you've joined this group

Session 1 is the same in all FOUNDATIONS studies. If you have recently used another FOUNDATIONS study with your current group, you may choose to do session 1 or merely to review it and then skip to session 2.

ON YOUR OWN   (30-60 minutes)

Most of us would like to love and be loved better than we already do and are. The FOUNDATIONS series revolves around three fundamental commands Jesus gave to His followers:

▶ Love God with all your heart, soul, mind, and strength (see Mark 12:30).
▶ Love one another as Jesus loves you (see John 13:34).
▶ Love your neighbor as yourself (see Mark 12:31).

In these verses, Jesus states the "big picture" of what the spiritual life is about. We love Him through worship, we love one another through

11

community, and we love others through service. We can depict this threefold lifestyle with the following set of concentric circles:

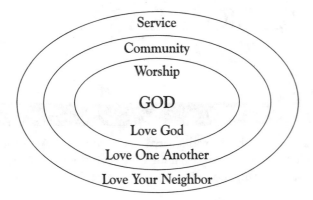

These three commands may be summarized in a single goal for the series:

To help you become a community—a small, closely knit group motivated and empowered to worship and serve God together.

Worship, community, and service form the structural backbone of the FOUNDATIONS process. They will direct your love toward God, toward the others in your group, and toward your neighbors (others not yet a part of your group). At the end of this study, you'll have a chance to summarize what you've learned about worship, community, and service, and to assess your progress as a group toward these three outcomes.

WORSHIP

God's commands about love show that He is vitally interested in relationships and that our relationship with Him should be our highest priority. Worship is the all-consuming, ongoing activity of heaven. We have the inexpressible privilege of joining in the cosmic worship of the King already taking place in the heavenly realm.

When we see God as He is and worship Him, the other areas of our lives begin to work themselves out. Drawing near to God's heart in spirit and truth will inevitably affect our relationships with others.

Hence, worship will become the centerpiece of your group experience. This concentration on God will set your little community apart from a mere discussion group or gathering of friends. While early sessions of this study will include suggestions for worship, feel free to use your entire group's creativity and experience under the leadership of the Holy Spirit as you come into God's presence session by session.

The essence of worship is turning our attention toward God, reflecting His glorious attributes back to Him, and agreeing with who He is and what He has done. God delights to reveal Himself more fully to us as we worship, to satisfy our hearts' desire for relationship with Him, and to give us help for our desperate needs.

God invites us to come to Him with our burdens, needs, joys, and heartaches. In reality, we cannot come to God without our burdens; they are part of who we are. Instead of denying the things on our hearts, we'll find it far more helpful to acknowledge them as fully as possible, commit them to God, then seek Him in His greatness for who He is.

1. When you think of worship, what ideas or images come to mind?
   ☐ lively music
   ☐ majestic hymns or choral works
   ☐ silence and solitude
   ☐ lengthy sermons
   ☐ performers and spectators
   ☐ communing with nature in the woods or by a stream
   ☐ all of life
   ☐ other:

2. On a scale of 1 to 10, how would you rate your most recent experience of worship in terms of how well it focused your heart on God's greatness? Why?

1	2	3	4	5	6	7	8	9	10
dry				okay					awesome

3. Does the idea of worship being the centerpiece of your group experience attract or trouble you? Why?

COMMUNITY

From a centered place of loving God, you'll move outward to loving the others in your group. This shared life is what the New Testament writers mean by *koinonia*: "fellowship," "communion," "partnership," "participation," "community."

> We saw it, we heard it, and now we're telling you so you can experience it along with us, this experience of communion with the Father and his Son, Jesus Christ. Our motive for writing is simply this: We want you to enjoy this, too. Your joy will double our joy! (1 John 1:3-4, MSG)

In the FOUNDATIONS series we assume that dynamic Christian community as described in the New Testament is not only possible but normative for us. When we fail to experience such relationships, we miss the fullness of life that God intends for us. While there are many spiritually important things one can and should do alone, an effective community contributes equally crucial ingredients of life. People in community can:

- ▶ encourage one another in good times and bad
- ▶ ask thoughtful questions when a member has a decision to make
- ▶ listen to God together
- ▶ learn how to pray together and for one another
- ▶ benefit from one another's insights into Scripture
- ▶ acquire a habit of reading the Bible
- ▶ practice loving their neighbors
- ▶ worship God together
- ▶ learn to communicate effectively and solve problems together
- ▶ learn to receive care from others
- ▶ experience the pleasure of helping another person grow

Community in these studies refers to a small group of 3 to 13 people who relate in a certain way. Community in this sense is very different from any organizational form or structure. Matthew 18:20 says, "For where there are two or three who have been joined together into my Name with the result that I am the common object of their faith, there I am in their midst."[1] The individuals together are seeking intimacy with God and fellowship with each other. *Koinonia* includes partnership, participation, and contribution. It implies communication and vulnerability. It is much more than just getting together and discussing some nonvolatile topic.

Jesus wanted His disciples to experience a unique relationship when they came together—unique in their love for and their unity with one another. When genuine love is present, a group has taken the first and biggest step toward real community. This process is not easy. Your group will probably have to resolve a number of relational issues on the road to biblical community.

4. What appeals to you about this description of community?

5. What questions or concerns do you have about this kind of community? Explain.

SERVICE

Any community focused on God loves to serve both believers and unbelievers, just as God does. How could it be otherwise? You'll find that as your group grows in worshiping God and loving one another, the members will intuitively know they need to be helping others. This will be natural.

What may not be natural is serving together as a team and serving the lost—both of which Jesus did and which His followers throughout history have done.

Most of us slowly abandon former friends and acquaintances when we join the kingdom of God. We're not comfortable anymore around those who do not share our new values. Our old friends no longer feel comfortable around us. Somehow we lose the ability Jesus had to be "a friend of tax collectors and 'sinners'" (Matthew 11:19). It is far easier for us to serve those within the kingdom of God than those more distant.

And if somehow we do seek to draw the lost toward Christ, we usually do so as individuals, rather than in partnership with other believers. Consequently, those who need the Savior never experience the powerful influence of a loving community.

The FOUNDATIONS studies will guide your group into these two dimensions: serving the lost and serving together. Serving does not exclusively mean explaining the gospel verbally. Loving our neighbor often translates into specific acts of compassionate service at home, neighborhood, or work. We often serve individually, but this FOUNDATIONS guide will focus your efforts on serving God's interests together. You will not be told what to do; you will not be pushed beyond your point of willing consent. Rather, you will decide together how to put what you are studying into practice outside your group.

6. What thoughts and feelings does this description of service raise for you?
   ☐ Excitement—I'm ready to go!
   ☐ Discomfort—The last thing I need is more on my "to-do" list.
   ☐ Anxiety—I did door-to-door witnessing several years ago and hated it. Will we have to do that again?
   ☐ Ambivalence—I have a strong desire to serve more, but I know it's not easy for me.
   ☐ Confusion—Isn't it good enough for us just to take care of each other for awhile?
   ☐ Relief—I'm glad this isn't just another navel-gazing group.
   ☐ Other (explain):

7. Is this statement true of you: "It is far easier for us to serve those within the kingdom of God than those more distant." If so, why do you think that is?

8. We have stated three priorities: loving God, loving others in the group, and loving others outside the group. What about loving yourself? Do you think this should be a priority ahead of any or all of these three? Explain your view.

 GROUP DISCOVERY (40 minutes)

Let's Warm Up (10 minutes)

Beginning with the leader, let each person take one minute to answer question 9.

9. Recall an important friendship from your childhood. Who was that friend, and what was special about that friendship? What bond kept you and that friend together?

Let's Talk (30 minutes)

10. Share your responses to questions 1-8 in the "On Your Own" section. Discuss any questions you have about the three big ideas stated there.

11. Discuss the following ground rules for your group. Feel free to change anything. The objective is for everyone to be content with the result, not for everyone to go along while harboring private reservations.
    ☐ Purpose: The reason our group exists is to become a community—a small, closely knit group motivated and empowered to worship and serve God.
    ☐ Participation: I am committed to participating in this community, to worshiping, and to serving others outside the group.
    ☐ Attendance: I will be here as often as possible. This group will be a priority.
    ☐ Ownership: I agree to share responsibility for our group goals.

☐ Confidentiality: I agree to keep here whatever is shared here.

☐ Accountability: I agree to give permission to the other group members to hold me accountable for goals I set for myself.

☐ Accessibility: I give group members permission to call me when they are in need—even in the middle of the night. My phone number is. . . .

12. Discuss the following discussion guidelines for your group. Again, feel free to change anything. The objective is for everyone to be pleased with the result, not for everyone to go along while harboring private reservations.

☐ Listen attentively. Ask questions only to enhance understanding. It is more important for an individual to express himself than for the group to understand fully.

☐ Respect the boundaries and comfort level of the one sharing. If details that you are dying to know don't come out, be willing to die. Allow the person sharing to choose the amount of information he or she discloses.

☐ Allow for the expression of emotions. Have a box of tissues available. If someone cries, don't be too quick to change the mood. Give adequate time for the person to compose and continue.

☐ Do not exhort, give advice, or teach. This is not a counseling session, but an opportunity for group members to share deep, inner feelings and responses with friends. Nothing will shut down a group like someone offering advice at such a time.

☐ Always affirm the person who has shared.

GROUP WORSHIP (15-30 minutes)

13. Pray that God would begin to reveal Himself in more of His majesty, power, and direction.

14. Read aloud together this portion of Psalm 89 (from *The Message*):

Your love, GOD, is my song, and I'll sing it!
    I'm forever telling everyone how faithful you are.

I'll never quit telling the story of your love—
   how you built the cosmos
   and guaranteed everything in it.
Your love has always been our lives' foundation,
   your fidelity has been the roof over our world.
You once said, "I joined forces with my chosen leader,
   I pledged my word to my servant, David, saying,
'Everyone descending from you is guaranteed life;
   I'll make your rule as solid and lasting as rock.'"

GOD! Let the cosmos praise your wonderful ways,
   the choir of holy angels sing anthems to your faithful ways!
Search high and low, scan skies and land,
   you'll find nothing and no one quite like GOD.
The holy angels are in awe before him;
   he looms immense and august over everyone around him.
GOD of the Angel Armies, who is like you,
   powerful and faithful from every angle?
You put the arrogant ocean in its place
   and calm its waves when they turn unruly.
You gave that old hag Egypt the back of your hand,
   you brushed off your enemies with a flick of your wrist.
You own the cosmos—you made everything in it,
   everything from atom to archangel.
You positioned the North and South Poles;
   the mountains Tabor and Hermon sing duets to you.
With your well-muscled arm and your grip of steel—
   nobody trifles with you!
The Right and Justice are the roots of your rule;
   Love and Truth are its fruits.
Blessed are the people who know the passwords of praise,
   who shout on parade in the bright presence of GOD.
Delighted, they dance all day long; they know
   who you are, what you do—they can't keep it quiet!
Your vibrant beauty has gotten inside us—
   you've been so good to us! We're walking on air!
All we are and have we owe to GOD,
   Holy God of Israel, our King! (Psalm 89:1-18, MSG)

19

15. Allow a moment of silence for everyone to focus on God. In worship, you have no agenda but to focus on Him.

16. Beginning with the leader, let each person thank God for one thing he or she learned in this session, or praise God for one aspect of Himself highlighted in your discussion. If you are comfortable doing so, allow for additional, spontaneous expressions of thanks and praise.

Optional

If you think your group might appreciate singing together, ask someone to lead with guitar or other instrument. If no one in your group has that skill, consider singing with a CD; some are now designed especially for small group worship. Be sure the person who leads worship understands that singing is only one aspect of worship, and that he or she should limit singing to the time allotted in your schedule.

---

1. Wuest, Kenneth S. *The New Testament: An Expanded Translation.* Grand Rapids, Mich.: Eerdmans, 1961.

2.

THE DYNAMICS OF COMMUNITY

How very good and pleasant it is when kindred live together in unity!

Psalm 133:1, NRSV

OVERVIEW

Relationships are at the heart of our Christian faith. Faith begins in a relationship with God and extends to our interaction with others in God's family. Finally, it flows out to our relationships with all of those we interact with from day to day.

How do we make our relationships function the way God intended? What does it mean to be the body of Christ? In this session, we will examine what the Bible says about how we should relate to one another. Your goal is to identify those traits that characterize the body of Christ and to begin exemplifying them in your group.

So, what's the big deal?
God designed us to live in relationship with Him and with others. What makes relationships work? How do we create such community?

ON YOUR OWN   (30-60 minutes)

1. How would you define community? What words come to mind?

The following passage from Acts describes how the first community of Christ's followers functioned.

> They devoted themselves to the apostles' teaching and to the fellowship, to the breaking of bread and to prayer. Everyone was filled with awe, and many wonders and miraculous signs were done by the apostles. All the believers were together and had everything in common. Selling their possessions and goods, they gave to anyone as he had need. Every day they continued to meet together in the temple courts. They broke bread in their homes and ate together with glad and sincere hearts, praising God and enjoying the favor of all the people. And the Lord added to their number daily those who were being saved.
> (Acts 2:42-47)

2. What were some of the things these people did together as a community?

3. How would you describe their relationships?

4. How do you think this community brought honor to God?

5. What obstacles would hinder a group from functioning like this today?

6. Do you think this level of relationship is possible in our culture today? What leads you to that conclusion?

7. What has been your best experience with a group or community? What were its positive qualities?

8. One of the goals for this study is for your group to become a community similar to the early believers (although not necessarily identical). What do you think about that goal? Does it seem desirable? Achievable? What makes you say that?

9. Review the rules for discussion found on page 18. How does following each of these guidelines build community?

10. a. Think about your expectations for this study. What are some of the things you hope to learn?

b. What kinds of relationships do you want to develop?

c. What needs would you like this group to meet?

For Further Study

"Fellowship" often brings to mind church potlucks and camping trips. But the Greek word *koinonia* means much more than that (see pages 14-15). It means a joint participation or partnership in a common activity or interest. What do the following passages reveal about the partnership in which Christians are engaged?

▶ Psalm 55:12-14   ▶ Philippians 3:10
▶ Philippians 1:4-5   ▶ Philippians 4:14-16
▶ Philippians 2:1-2   ▶ 1 John 1:3-7

 GROUP DISCOVERY   (50-90 minutes)

Let's Warm Up (10 minutes)

11. Who was your first friend? What do you remember about that friendship?

24

Let's Talk (30-50 minutes)

12. Discuss the "On Your Own" questions. What did you learn about community? About the early believers?

13. Share your definitions of community with each other. Take a few minutes to combine your definitions and come up with a phrase that defines community for your group.

14. We all have expectations about our relationships. In the "On Your Own" section you identified some of your expectations for this group. Pick one or two of your expectations to share with the group. Remember that it's nearly impossible for others to meet your expectations (or for you to meet theirs) if those expectations aren't communicated clearly. Think of these expectations as requests that are open to negotiation, rather than as demands.

In his first letter to the Corinthians, Paul explained how believers should relate to one another. He compared the body of believers to an actual body—an analogy we can all relate to. Have someone read the following passage aloud.

> You can easily enough see how this kind of thing works by looking no further than your own body. Your body has many parts—limbs, organs, cells—but no matter how many parts you can name, you're still one body. It's exactly the same with Christ. By means of his one Spirit, we all said goodbye to our partial and piecemeal lives. We each used to independently call our own shots, but then we entered into a large

and integrated life in which *he* has the final say in everything. (This is what we proclaimed in word and action when we were baptized.) Each of us is now a part of his resurrection body, refreshed and sustained at one fountain—his Spirit—where we all come to drink. The old labels we once used to identify ourselves—labels like Jew or Greek, slave or free—are no longer useful. We need something larger, more comprehensive.

I want you to think about how all this makes you more significant, not less. A body isn't just a single part blown up into something huge. It's all the different-but-similar parts arranged and functioning together. If Foot said, "I'm not elegant like Hand, embellished with rings; I guess I don't belong to this body," would that make it so? If Ear said, "I'm not beautiful like Eye, limpid and expressive; I don't deserve a place on the head," would you want to remove it from the body? If the body was all eye, how could it hear? If all ear, how could it smell? As it is, we see that God has carefully placed each part of the body right where he wanted it.

But I also want you to think about how this keeps your significance from getting blown up into self-importance. For no matter how significant you are, it is only because of what you are a *part* of. An enormous eye or a gigantic hand wouldn't be a body, but a monster. What we have is one body with many parts, each its proper size and in its proper place. No part is important on its own. Can you imagine Eye telling Hand, "Get lost; I don't need you"? Or, Head telling Foot, "You're fired; your job has been phased out"? As a matter of fact, in practice it works the other way—the "lower" the part, the more basic, and therefore necessary. You can live without an eye, for instance, but not without a stomach. When it's a part of your own body you are concerned with, it makes *no* difference whether the part is visible or clothed, higher or lower. You give it dignity and honor just as it is, without comparisons. If anything, you have more concern for the lower parts than the higher. If you had to choose, wouldn't you prefer good digestion to full-bodied hair?

The way God designed our bodies is a model for understanding our lives together as a church: every part dependent on every other part, the parts we mention and the parts we don't, the parts we see and the parts we don't. If one part hurts, every other part is involved in the hurt, and in the healing. If one part flourishes, every other part enters into the exuberance.

You are Christ's body—that's who you are! You must never forget this. Only as you accept your part of that body does your "part" mean anything.
(1 Corinthians 12:12-27, MSG)

15. According to Paul, in what ways is the community of believers like a human body?

16. What are some of the mistakes Paul says people make when they don't understand they are part of a body?

17. How does Paul say the parts of the body should relate to each other?

18. How does it make you feel to know that you are part of a body?

19. In what ways is your group like a body?

20. To what degree (a lot, a little, or not much) would you say each of the following statements is true of you?
    ☐ I understand the unique abilities I bring to this group.
    ☐ I understand the unique abilities each of the other members brings to this group.
    ☐ I highly value what I bring to this group.
    ☐ I highly value what each member brings to this group.
    ☐ I hurt when others in the group hurt.
    ☐ I celebrate when others in the group are flourishing.
    ☐ Other (please explain):

Let's Act (15 minutes)
21. What are the implications of this discussion for these three aspects of your group life:

    ☐ Your worship

    ☐ Your relationships with each other

    ☐ Your responsibilities/relationships with others (neighbors, coworkers, family, seekers, new believers, disciples, enemies)

22. Which, if any, of the qualities and practices of the early believers would you like your group to adopt? (Do your best to get specific, then agree on a time frame.)

 GROUP WORSHIP (15-30 minutes)

23. Read Psalm 133 together as a group.

How wonderful, how beautiful,
    when brothers and sisters get along!
It's like costly anointing oil
    flowing down head and beard,
Flowing down Aaron's beard,
    flowing down the collar of his priestly robes.
It's like the dew on Mount Hermon
    flowing down the slopes of Zion.
Yes, that's where GOD commands the blessing,
    ordains eternal life. (Psalm 133:1-3, MSG)

24. If your group is so inclined, sing an appropriate hymn or chorus, then close in prayer. Thank God for the relationships within your group and for the opportunity to become a community that honors Him. Ask Him to guide your group, to build friendships among you, and to draw you closer to Him. Share any requests and commit to pray for each other throughout the upcoming week.

3.
LEARNING TO LOVE ONE ANOTHER

"And so I am giving a new commandment to you now—
love each other just as much as I love you. Your strong
love for each other will prove to the world that you are
my disciples."

—*John 13:34-35,* TLB

OVERVIEW

Loving some people seems to come naturally, while loving others seems possible only with supernatural help. In reality, though, deep and consistent love that sees beyond one's own needs is always supernatural. Yet love is an integral part of the community God wants believers to experience—something we must work on diligently.

Love is a command. We are to love our neighbors, our enemies, and our friends. With attitudes and feelings that can change in an instant, how can we learn to love such diverse groups genuinely and with consistency?

In this session, we will look at some of God's commands about love. We'll see how our love for others must flow from our love from God. Your goal is to gain a clearer understanding of love and to identify areas where you can learn to love more consistently.

So, what's the big deal?

God commands us to love each other—regardless of our feelings and attitudes. How can we learn to love the way God commands?

ON YOUR OWN (30-60 minutes)

1. How would you define love?

2. Perhaps the best-known Bible passage on love is found in 1 Corinthians 13. Underline the words that stand out to you.

If I speak with human eloquence and angelic ecstasy but don't love, I'm nothing but the creaking of a rusty gate.
     If I speak God's Word with power, revealing all his mysteries and making everything plain as day, and if I have faith that says to a mountain, "Jump," and it jumps, but I don't love, I'm nothing.
     If I give everything I own to the poor and even go to the stake to be burned as a martyr, but I don't love, I've gotten nowhere. So, no matter what I say, what I believe, and what I do, I'm bankrupt without love.

Love never gives up.
Love cares more for others than for self.
Love doesn't want what it doesn't have.
Love doesn't strut,
Doesn't have a swelled head,
Doesn't force itself on others,
Isn't always "me first,"
Doesn't fly off the handle,
Doesn't keep score of the sins of others,
Doesn't revel when others grovel,
Takes pleasure in the flowering of truth,
Puts up with anything,
Trusts God always,
Always looks for the best,

Never looks back,
But keeps going to the end.

Love never dies. (1 Corinthians 13:1-8, MSG)

3. Paul describes love by explaining what love is and isn't. Reread the passage, filling in the chart below.

WHAT LOVE IS	WHAT LOVE ISN'T

4. a. Think about how you love those around you. What are some characteristics of love that you do well?

   b. What are some of the things that you could do better?

5. How do you think a person grows deeper and more consistent in these habits? What does the process look like? (For instance, what does God do? What does the person need to do?)

The apostle John also describes love and its importance in God's family.

> For this is the original message we heard: We should love
> each other.
> We must not be like Cain, who joined the Evil One and
> then killed his brother. And why did he kill him? Because
> he was deep in the practice of evil, while the acts of his
> brother were righteous. So don't be surprised, friends, when
> the world hates you. This has been going on a long time.
> The way we know we've been transferred from death to
> life is that we love our brothers and sisters. Anyone who
> doesn't love is as good as dead. Anyone who hates a brother
> or sister is a murderer, and you know very well that eternal
> life and murder don't go together.
> This is how we've come to understand and experience
> love: Christ sacrificed his life for us. This is why we ought to
> live sacrificially for our fellow believers, and not just be out
> for ourselves. If you see some brother or sister in need and
> have the means to do something about it but turn a cold
> shoulder and do nothing, what happens to God's love? It
> disappears. And you made it disappear.
> My dear children, let's not just talk about love; let's
> practice real love. (1 John 3:11-18, MSG)

6. How does John define love?

7. What do you think John means when he says that we make God's love disappear by refusing to meet another's needs?

8. What are some ways we can "live sacrificially for our fellow believers"?

9. How does this kind of love affect our relationships with unbelievers?

10. Think of someone you have difficulty loving. What do you think would happen if you began living sacrificially for that person?

 GROUP DISCOVERY (50-90 minutes)

Let's Warm Up (10 minutes)
11. What are some of the things that make you feel loved?

Let's Talk (30-50 minutes)
12. Discuss the "On Your Own" questions. What did you learn about love? About yourself?

13. Why do you think it's harder to love some people than others?

Our love for others must flow from our love from God—the two are vitally linked. The apostle John explains how this works. Have someone read the passage below out loud.

My beloved friends, let us continue to love each other since love comes from God. Everyone who loves is born of God and experiences a relationship with God. The person who refuses to love doesn't know the first thing about God, because God *is* love—so you can't know him if you don't love. This is how God showed his love for us: God sent his only Son into the world so we might live through him. This is the kind of love we are talking about—not that we once upon a time loved God, but that he loved us and sent his Son as a sacrifice to clear away our sins and the damage they've done to our relationship with God.

My dear, dear friends, if God loved us like this, we certainly ought to love each other. No one has seen God, ever. But if we love one another, God dwells deeply within us, and his love becomes complete in us—perfect love!

This is how we know we're living steadily and deeply in him, and he in us: He's given us life from his life, from his very own Spirit. Also, we've seen for ourselves and continue to state openly that the Father sent his Son as Savior of the world. Everyone who confesses that Jesus is God's Son participates continuously in an intimate relationship with God. We know it so well, we've embraced it heart and soul, this love that comes from God.

God is love. When we take up permanent residence in a life of love, we live in God and God lives in us. This way, love has the run of the house, becomes at home and mature in us, so that we're free of worry on Judgment Day—our standing in the world is identical with Christ's. There is no room in love for fear. Well-formed love banishes fear. Since fear is crippling, a fearful life—fear of death, fear of judgment—is one not yet fully formed in love.

We, though, are going to love—love and be loved. First we were loved, now we love. He loved us first.

If anyone boasts, "I love God," and goes right on hating

his brother or sister, thinking nothing of it, he is a liar. If he won't love the person he can see, how can he love the God he can't see? The command we have from Christ is blunt: Loving God includes loving people. You've got to love both. (1 John 4:7-21, MSG)

14. What are some of the key words that stand out to you from this passage?

15. According to John, how has God shown His love for us?

16. Over time, we can get used to the notion that Christ died for us— we take it for granted and it ceases to move us. What do you feel right now when you think about God's demonstration of love?

17. Do you think all love comes from God? What leads you to that conclusion?

18. Why do you think John mentions fear in his explanation of love?

19. John says that if we can't love the people we see, we certainly can't love God, whom we can't see. Why would that be?

Some people are hard to love. Others are next to impossible. But if we love God, we must love them too. Jesus gave some helpful instruction on how we can grow in love for those we don't even like.

> "To you who are ready for the truth, I say this: Love your enemies. Let them bring out the best in you, not the worst. When someone gives you a hard time, respond with the energies of prayer for that person. If someone slaps you in the face, stand there and take it. If someone grabs your shirt, giftwrap your best coat and make a present of it. If someone takes unfair advantage of you, use the occasion to practice the servant life. No more tit-for-tat stuff. Live generously.
>
> "Here is a simple rule of thumb for behavior: Ask yourself what you want people to do for you; then grab the initiative and do it for *them*! If you only love the lovable, do you expect a pat on the back? Run-of-the-mill sinners do that. If you only help those who help you, do you expect a medal? Garden-variety sinners do that. If you only give for what you hope to get out of it, do you think that's charity? The stingiest of pawnbrokers does that.
>
> "I tell you, love your enemies. Help and give without expecting a return. You'll never—I promise—regret it. Live out this God-created identity the way our Father lives toward us, generously and graciously, even when we're at our worst. Our Father is kind; you be kind."
> (Luke 6:27-36, MSG)

20. What reasons does Jesus give for loving our enemies?

21. When Jesus says that we'll never regret loving our enemies, what do you think He means?

22. Think about the definitions of love you've read in 1 Corinthians and 1 John. What does it mean to love an enemy? (For example, does it mean having warm, affectionate feelings?)

23. At the beginning of this passage, Jesus speaks of being "ready" for the truth. In what sense does one need to be ready to receive this truth about loving enemies?

Let's Act (15-30 minutes)

24. What are some ways in which you could show love for each other in your group?

25. What about to those outside your group?

26. From this lesson, is there anything you sense the Holy Spirit directing your group to do?

27. Design your own time of worship based on the material in this session.

Let's Listen to God (15 minutes)

Throughout this study guide the question, "What do you think the Holy Spirit is saying to your group about . . . ?" is raised. Perhaps it seems presumptuous to claim to know what the Spirit is saying. Perhaps you are confident that you know, or maybe you are willing to settle for what you think the Spirit *ought* to be saying to your group.

Listening to the Spirit's voice is a skill your group can develop over time. It requires discipline and the willingness to cultivate certain attitudes and take certain risks. As you begin your time of listening to God, read aloud the following commitments. These are not once-for-all-time commitments; each one will require a process of commitment and recommitment by each group member.

▶ We acknowledge our own agendas, plans, philosophies, ideas, and paradigms, and we determine not to let them interfere with our relationship with God or with each other. We may not get this right all the time, but will keep it in mind every week as we meet.

▶ We commit ourselves to being open, honest, vulnerable, available, and transparent. Of course, if we're going to do this for real, we will have to deal with the relationship tensions and conflicts that arise. The result will be the beginning of authentic relationships.

▶ We present ourselves to God in humility, poverty of spirit, brokenness, contrition, and submission. God says He is near to these kinds of persons (Isaiah 57:15, 66:2). The prophet Azariah told the king and people of Judah:

"The LORD is with you when you are with him. If you seek him, he will be found by you, but if you forsake him, he will forsake you. For a long time Israel was without the true God. . . . But in their distress they turned to the LORD, the God of Israel, and sought him, and he was found by them." (2 Chronicles 15:1-4)

Your agenda for this time of listening to God is to try to hear what God is saying through each group member as you share your thoughts on the following questions. Your challenge is to listen to God while talking to each other. Take a moment for silent prayer, then spend about fifteen minutes on the following:

28. After reading aloud the preceding three commitments, discuss what you sense the Holy Spirit communicating to your group about the following areas.

    ☐ Your worship and relationship with God

    ☐ Your relationships with each other

    ☐ Your relationships with those outside this group

Take a moment to close this conversation in prayer.

41

4.

DEALING WITH CONFLICT

If it is possible, as far as it depends on you, live at peace with everyone.

—Romans 12:18

OVERVIEW

Being part of a community and having relationships with others means dealing with conflict. Even the disciples argued about who would be the greatest in Christ's coming kingdom. Differences of opinions, personalities, and ideas will occur. How we handle them says a lot about our maturity and walk with God.

The Bible addresses all areas of life, even how to deal with difficult situations and people when they arise. In this session, we'll examine what the Bible says about conflict and discover how to resolve it. Your goal is to gain a clearer understanding of why conflict happens and how to deal with it biblically.

So, what's the big deal?

If we interact with others, conflict is inevitable. Some of us have had bad experiences with conflict and feel it is inherently unChristian. Are there ways of dealing with it that are not destructive to relationships?

ON YOUR OWN   (30-60 minutes)

1. What are some of the words that come to mind when you think of conflict?

2. How would you define conflict?

3. What is your typical response to conflict? Do you . . .
   - ☐ ignore it and try to work around it, hoping it will go away?
   - ☐ defend yourself no matter what?
   - ☐ confront the issues (or the person) head on?
   - ☐ pray before taking any action?
   - ☐ hide and hope the other person will forget?
   - ☐ admit it if you're wrong?
   - ☐ seek counsel from the Holy Spirit?
   - ☐ other (please explain):

4. What are some of the causes of conflicts you've had recently?

The apostle James didn't mince words when describing the conflict we often experience:

> What causes fights and quarrels among you? Don't they come from your desires that battle within you? You want something but don't get it. You kill and covet, but you cannot have what you want. You quarrel and fight. You do not have, because you do not ask God. When you ask, you do not receive, because you ask with wrong motives, that you may spend what you get on your pleasures.
> You adulterous people, don't you know that friendship with the world is hatred toward God? Anyone who chooses to be a friend of the world becomes an enemy of God. Or

do you think Scripture says without reason that the spirit he caused to live in us envies intensely? But he gives us more grace. That is why Scripture says:

> "God opposes the proud
> but gives grace to the humble."

Submit yourselves, then, to God. Resist the devil, and he will flee from you. Come near to God and he will come near to you. Wash your hands, you sinners, and purify your hearts, you double-minded. Grieve, mourn and wail. Change your laughter to mourning and your joy to gloom. Humble yourselves before the Lord, and he will lift you up.

Brothers, do not slander one another. Anyone who speaks against his brother or judges him speaks against the law and judges it. When you judge the law, you are not keeping it, but sitting in judgment on it. (James 4:1-11)

5. According to James, what are some of the things that cause conflict?

6. What does James say is the solution to these fights and quarrels?

7. James says that our motives are often wrong when we ask God for things. How can we make sure our motives are pure when making requests?

8. How would you define "humility"?

9. What does it mean that God will lift us up if we humble ourselves?

10. Why do you think James urges his readers to "grieve, mourn and wail"?

11. What is slander?

12. How is it related to judgment?

13. What are some steps you can take to act more humbly in the midst of conflict?

For Further Study

Spend some time this week thinking about how you typically resolve conflicts, reviewing question 3 above. You may even want to ask others who know you well and whose counsel you trust. Also, think about why you handle conflict in that way. Most of us learned our style of handling conflict from our families, not from the Bible. How did the various members of your family deal with conflict when you were growing up, and how has that affected you?

 GROUP DISCOVERY (50-90 minutes)

Let's Warm Up (10 minutes)

14. Conflicts don't always center around serious subjects. What are some of the silly things you've had arguments about with others?

Let's Talk (30-50 minutes)

15. Discuss the "On Your Own" questions. What did you learn about conflict and its causes? About yourself and how you handle conflict?

Love has a lot to do with handling conflict well. As we learn to love those around us (even those we don't like), dealing with conflict has the potential to get easier.

In his letter to the Romans, the apostle Paul gives some good advice for dealing with conflict in a loving manner.

> Love must be sincere. Hate what is evil; cling to what is good. Be devoted to one another in brotherly love. Honor one another above yourselves. Never be lacking in zeal, but keep your spiritual fervor, serving the Lord. Be joyful in hope, patient in affliction, faithful in prayer. Share with God's people who are in need. Practice hospitality.

Bless those who persecute you; bless and do not curse. Rejoice with those who rejoice; mourn with those who mourn. Live in harmony with one another. Do not be proud, but be willing to associate with people of low position. Do not be conceited.

Do not repay anyone evil for evil. Be careful to do what is right in the eyes of everybody. If it is possible, as far as it depends on you, live at peace with everyone. Do not take revenge, my friends, but leave room for God's wrath, for it is written: "It is mine to avenge; I will repay," says the Lord. On the contrary:

"If your enemy is hungry, feed him;
   if he is thirsty, give him something to drink.
In doing this, you will heap burning coals on his head."

Do not be overcome by evil, but overcome evil with good. (Romans 12:9-21)

16. What responses to evil does Paul encourage?

17. How does Paul say we should handle conflict?

18. Paul urges us to live at peace with everyone, as far as it depends on us. Why do you suppose living at peace is so important?

19. After reading the following scenario, describe how you think Janet should go about seeking to live at peace with Rachel. What would be a godly and wise way to handle this conflict?

> Janet and Rachel work in the same department and are potential candidates for the same promotion, should that position ever become available. Rachel has a habit of undercutting Janet—minimizing her performance and maximizing her flaws when Rachel is speaking with coworkers or managers. Janet is angry about this.

20. How do you think sincerity, honor, and love affect conflict?

21. What's the difference between sincere love and insincere love? What do they look like?

22. What difference does it make to you to know that God will repay the wrongs done to you?

Let's Act (15 minutes)

23. Handling conflict with love isn't easy. Have you had an experience where you were able to resolve conflict in the way that Paul describes? If so, describe it.

24. How can this group help you as you face conflict with others?

25. Based on this study, decide how your group will face and process conflicts when they arise.

GROUP WORSHIP   (15-30 minutes)

26. The opposite of conflict is peace. Jesus has promised us His peace. Spend a few minutes meditating on the verses below and then share any observations you may have.

> "Peace I leave with you; my peace I give you. I do not give to you as the world gives. Do not let your hearts be troubled and do not be afraid." (John 14:27)

> "I have told you these things, so that in me you may have peace. In this world you will have trouble. But take heart! I have overcome the world." (John 16:33)

27. If your group is so inclined, sing an appropriate hymn or chorus and close in prayer. Then, divide into pairs. Share any conflict

you're currently experiencing, and spend time praying for each other. Commit to pray for each other during the upcoming week and to follow-up on these requests at your next meeting.

5.
LEARNING TO FORGIVE

*Bear with each other and forgive whatever grievances
you may have against one another. Forgive as the Lord
forgave you.*

—Colossians 3:13

OVERVIEW

Even when conflict is resolved, feelings of anger and
bitterness can remain. A mere thought of it can bring back the strong
emotions felt during the heat of the argument. Even when forgiveness
has been asked for and given, we can't forget the hurt we've felt. How
do we make those feelings go away for good?

In this session, we'll examine forgiveness. We'll learn what forgiveness is, when it's necessary, and what the Bible has to say about it. Your
goal is to understand why forgiveness is an essential ingredient in the
Christian life and to identify any of your relationships where forgiveness is needed.

So, what's the big deal?
Jesus said that we must forgive in order to be forgiven. What does that
really mean, and how can we know when to give forgiveness and when
to ask for it?

ON YOUR OWN   (30-60 minutes)

1. How would you define forgiveness?

2. Think about asking for or being asked for forgiveness. How often does it happen to you?
   - ☐ Regularly—a couple of times a month
   - ☐ Often—at least once a month
   - ☐ Every once in a while—several times a year
   - ☐ Rarely—once a year
   - ☐ Hardly ever—once or twice every few years
   - ☐ Other (please explain):

3. When was the last time you asked someone for forgiveness? Describe the situation.

4. When was the last time someone asked for your forgiveness? Describe the situation.

When the disciples asked Jesus how they were to pray, forgiveness was a key point in His instruction.

> "This, then, is how you should pray:
>
> "'Our Father in heaven,
> hallowed be your name,
> your kingdom come,
> your will be done
>   on earth as it is in heaven.
> Give us today our daily bread.

Forgive us our debts,
    as we also have forgiven our debtors.
And lead us not into temptation,
but deliver us from the evil one.'

"For if you forgive men when they sin against you, your heavenly Father will also forgive you. But if you do not forgive men their sins, your Father will not forgive your sins." (Matthew 6:9-15)

5. How does Jesus say we should forgive?

6. Why should we forgive those who sin against us?

7. Why do you think Jesus included extra instruction about forgiveness after giving the disciples the Lord's Prayer?

8. How do you respond to the idea that God won't forgive you if you don't forgive others?

Sometimes it seems that the same people wrong us over and over, constantly expecting us to forgive them. The apostle Peter asked the same question we find ourselves asking in that situation: "How long do I have to put up with this?"

Then Peter came to Jesus and asked, "Lord, how many times shall I forgive my brother when he sins against me? Up to seven times?"

Jesus answered, "I tell you, not seven times, but seventy-seven times.

"Therefore, the kingdom of heaven is like a king who wanted to settle accounts with his servants. As he began the settlement, a man who owed him ten thousand talents was brought to him. Since he was not able to pay, the master ordered that he and his wife and his children and all that he had be sold to repay the debt.

"The servant fell on his knees before him. 'Be patient with me,' he begged, 'and I will pay back everything.' The servant's master took pity on him, canceled the debt and let him go.

"But when that servant went out, he found one of his fellow servants who owed him a hundred denarii. He grabbed him and began to choke him. 'Pay back what you owe me!' he demanded.

"His fellow servant fell to his knees and begged him, 'Be patient with me, and I will pay you back.'

"But he refused. Instead, he went off and had the man thrown into prison until he could pay the debt. When the other servants saw what had happened, they were greatly distressed and went and told their master everything that had happened.

"Then the master called the servant in. 'You wicked servant,' he said, 'I canceled all that debt of yours because you begged me to. Shouldn't you have had mercy on your fellow servant just as I had on you?' In anger his master turned him over to the jailers to be tortured, until he should pay back all he owed.

"This is how my heavenly Father will treat each of you

unless you forgive your brother from your heart."
(Matthew 18:21-35)

9. Describe a time when you felt pushed to the "forgiveness limit."

10. When Jesus said we should forgive someone seventy-seven times, what do you think He was really telling Peter?

11. To explain His outrageous standard of forgiveness, Jesus told a story.

   a. Who are the main characters in the story?

   b. With which character do you most identify? Why?

12. What is the point of this story?

13. What does forgiveness from the heart look like?

14. Imagine being Peter. What list of objections might Peter raise to this blanket instruction about forgiving someone seventy-seven times from the heart?

For Further Study

Jesus emphasizes over and over that our capacity to forgive is proportional to our awareness of the forgiveness we have received. Would you say you have been forgiven much or little? Read Luke 7:36-50, and consider whether you identify more with the prostitute or with Simon, the respectable religious leader. What does this story tell you about the connection between forgiveness and love?

 GROUP DISCOVERY (50-90 minutes)

Let's Warm Up (10 minutes)

15. What's something that you would have difficulty forgiving?

Let's Talk (30-50 minutes)

16. Discuss the "On Your Own" questions. What did you learn about forgiveness?

17. Share your definitions of forgiveness. Take a few minutes to combine them into a definition the whole group agrees on.

Sometimes people ask for forgiveness, but often they don't even admit they did something wrong. What if someone wrongs you and doesn't seek reconciliation or forgiveness? Jesus' disciples had some of the same questions we do. Have someone read each of these passages aloud.

> "If your brother sins, rebuke him, and if he repents, forgive him. If he sins against you seven times in a day, and seven times comes back to you and says, 'I repent,' forgive him." (Luke 17:3-4)

> "If your brother sins against you, go and show him his fault, just between the two of you. If he listens to you, you have won your brother over. But if he will not listen, take one or two others along, so that 'every matter may be established by the testimony of two or three witnesses.' If he refuses to listen to them, tell it to the church; and if he refuses to listen even to the church, treat him as you would a pagan or a tax collector." (Matthew 18:15-17)

18. These statements add some conditions to the blanket instructions about forgiveness you studied on your own. In these passages, what must someone do to receive forgiveness?

19. To "repent" means to change one's mind, to go beyond one's previous thinking, or to change direction. Jesus tells us to forgive if someone "repents" seven times in one day for the same offense. What evidence of repentance do you think Jesus would say warrants forgiveness?

59

20. When someone doesn't listen when confronted about sin, Jesus says to treat him or her as "a pagan or a tax collector." What do you think He means?

21. Are there ever times when forgiveness is not called for?

22. The instructions found in Matthew 18:15-17 (printed above) seem to establish conditions for forgiveness. On the other hand, the story found in Matthew 18:21-35 that you studied in the "On Your Own" section speaks of incredible generosity. How do you reconcile the two? What is the full picture of what Jesus says about the forgiveness?

23. If you were going to establish guidelines for forgiveness, what would they be?

Let's Act (15 minutes)
24. Unfortunately, forgiveness doesn't come naturally to us. What are some ways in which you can become more forgiving?

25. Are there any people whom you need to confront with sin, to whom you need to offer forgiveness, or from whom you need to ask for forgiveness? If so, what steps will you take this week to do so?

26. How can this group support you?

 GROUP WORSHIP (15-30 minutes)

27. Read Psalm 103 out loud together.

Praise the LORD, O my soul;
    all my inmost being, praise his holy name.
Praise the LORD, O my soul,
    and forget not all his benefits—
who forgives all your sins
    and heals all your diseases,
who redeems your life from the pit
    and crowns you with love and compassion,
who satisfies your desires with good things
    so that your youth is renewed like the eagle's.

The LORD works righteousness
    and justice for all the oppressed.

He made known his ways to Moses,
    his deeds to the people of Israel:
The LORD is compassionate and gracious,
    slow to anger, abounding in love.
He will not always accuse,
    nor will he harbor his anger forever;
he does not treat us as our sins deserve

or repay us according to our iniquities.
For as high as the heavens are above the earth,
    so great is his love for those who fear him;
as far as the east is from the west,
    so far has he removed our transgressions from us.
As a father has compassion on his children,
    so the LORD has compassion on those who fear him;
for he knows how we are formed,
    he remembers that we are dust.
As for man, his days are like grass,
    he flourishes like a flower of the field;
the wind blows over it and it is gone,
    and its place remembers it no more.
But from everlasting to everlasting
    the LORD's love is with those who fear him,
    and his righteousness with their children's children—
with those who keep his covenant
    and remember to obey his precepts.

The LORD has established his throne in heaven,
    and his kingdom rules over all.

Praise the LORD, you his angels,
    you mighty ones who do his bidding,
    who obey his word.
Praise the LORD, all his heavenly hosts,
    you his servants who do his will.
Praise the LORD, all his works
    everywhere in his dominion.

Praise the LORD, O my soul. (Psalm 103:1-22)

Let's Listen to God (15 minutes)

28. After reading aloud the three commitments listed on pages 40-41, discuss what you sense the Holy Spirit is communicating to your group about the following areas.

☐ Your worship and relationship with God

☐ Your relationships with each other

☐ Your relationships with those outside this group

Take a moment to close this conversation in prayer.

6.
COMMUNITY AND THE WORK OF THE HOLY SPIRIT

Since this is the kind of life we have chosen, the life of the
Spirit, let us make sure that we do not just hold it as an
idea in our heads or a sentiment in our hearts, but work
out its implications in every detail of our lives.

—Galatians 5:25, MSG

OVERVIEW

When we place our trust in God we begin a new life in Him. In Romans, Paul describes this as putting off the old life (or self) and putting on a new one. The Holy Spirit is our guide in this new life, giving us direction and insight into how we should live.

This new life, "the life in the Spirit," is designed to be lived in community with others. In fact, the evidence of the Spirit's work in us—the fruit of the Spirit—is visible only as we interact with other people. It is in relationships with other people, in community, that we find opportunities for the Holy Spirit to guide us and produce fruit in our lives.

In this session, we will examine the fruit of the Spirit and how He influences our relationships. Your goal is to understand how the Holy Spirit works and to continue to become a community that reflects the Spirit's activity.

So, what's the big deal?
For many of us, much of the time we spend with God is spent alone. Why, then, is community so important to the work of the Holy Spirit? How does the Holy Spirit affect our relationships?

1. Describe the Holy Spirit as you know Him. Who is He? What is His role in your life?

One of the things that usually comes to mind when we talk about the Holy Spirit is the fruit Paul discusses in Galatians:

> But the fruit of the Spirit is love, joy, peace, patience, kindness, goodness, faithfulness, gentleness, and self-control. Against such things there is no law. Those who belong to Christ Jesus have crucified the sinful nature with its passions and desires. Since we live by the Spirit, let us keep in step with the Spirit. Let us not become conceited, provoking and envying each other. (Galatians 5:22-26)

2. The word "fruit" here is singular, but it has nine qualities. Underline them. Why would it be impossible to exercise these qualities in isolation from other people?

3. Why do you suppose Paul described these qualities as "fruit"? What does that word picture suggest to you?

4. What do you think Paul means when he says that "against such things there is no law"?

5. Why do you suppose Paul included a warning about conceit when talking about the fruit of the Spirit?

6. What does it mean to you that your old nature and desires have been crucified?

7. Is there an area of your life—especially one that affects your relationships—that needs to be crucified?

Sometimes it's helpful to read a passage of Scripture in a different version. Read the same verses from Galatians again, this time from *The Message*.

> But what happens when we live God's way? He brings gifts into our lives, much the same way that fruit appears in an orchard—things like affection for others, exuberance about life, serenity. We develop a willingness to stick with things, a sense of compassion in the heart, and a conviction that a basic holiness permeates things and people. We find ourselves involved in loyal commitments, not needing to force our way in life, able to marshal and direct our energies wisely.
>
> Legalism is helpless in bringing this about; it only gets in the way. Among those who belong to Christ, everything connected with getting our own way and mindlessly responding to what everyone else calls necessities is killed off for good—crucified.
>
> Since this is the kind of life we have chosen, the life of the Spirit, let us make sure that we do not just hold it as an

idea in our heads or a sentiment in our hearts, but work out its implications in every detail of our lives. That means we will not compare ourselves with each other as if one of us were better and another worse. We have far more interesting things to do with our lives. Each of us is an original. (Galatians 5:22-26, MSG)

8. What new insights into the fruit do you get from this version?

9. What does it mean to live the life of the Spirit in "every detail of our lives"?

10. How can others help or hinder your growth in manifesting the fruit of the Spirit?

11. How would your relationships change if you consistently evidenced the qualities that Paul describes?

12. Which aspect of the fruit of the Spirit is least evident in your relationships?

13. What steps can you take toward manifesting that quality more consistently?

For Further Study

Read Romans 8:1-27, looking for references to the Holy Spirit. What does the Spirit do? What do we do in response to the Spirit? How should these actions and responses affect our relationships?

 GROUP DISCOVERY (50-90 minutes)

Let's Warm Up (10 minutes)

14. What are some of the qualities that you look for in a friend?

Let's Talk (30-50 minutes)

15. Discuss the "On Your Own" questions. What did you learn about the Holy Spirit and His work? Yourself? Your relationships?

The Holy Spirit produces fruit or results in our lives. That fruit affects how we live and relate to each other. Paul wrote to the Ephesian church from prison and explained what relationships ruled by the Spirit look like. He said, "Make every effort to keep the unity of the Spirit through the bond of peace" (Ephesians 4:3).

16. What do you think "the unity of the Spirit" is?

Here is the context of this statement, as translated in *The Message*. Have someone read it aloud.

> In light of all this, here's what I want you to do. While I'm locked up here, a prisoner for the Master, I want you to get out there and walk—better yet, run!—on the road God called you to travel. I don't want any of you sitting around on your hands. I don't want anyone strolling off, down some path that goes nowhere. And mark that you do this with humility and discipline—not in fits and starts, but steadily, pouring yourselves out for each other in acts of love, alert at noticing differences and quick at mending fences.
>
> You were all called to travel on the same road and in the same direction, so stay together, both outwardly and inwardly. You have one Master, one faith, one baptism, one God and Father of all, who rules over all, works through all, and is present in all. Everything you are and think and do is permeated with Oneness.
>
> But that doesn't mean you should all look and speak and act the same. Out of the generosity of Christ, each of us is given his own gift. . . . He handed out gifts above and below, filled heaven with his gifts, filled earth with his gifts. He handed out gifts of apostle, prophet, evangelist, and pastor-teacher to train Christians in skilled servant work, working within Christ's body, the church, until we're all moving rhythmically and easily with each other, efficient and graceful in response to God's Son, fully mature adults, fully developed within and without, fully alive like Christ. (Ephesians 4:1-7,10-13, MSG)

17. What picture of the unity of the Spirit does this passage paint? What does it say about relationships among God's people?

18. Why do you think Paul notes that we are to pour ourselves out for each other in acts of love—*steadily*?

19. Why is unity (or in this version, staying together) so important?

20. How is staying together on the same path possible?

21. Paul says that as a community of believers we are to be "permeated with Oneness." To what degree do you think that describes your group? What factors contribute to that?

22. Paul is also describing how all believers everywhere should act. What role does the Holy Spirit play in our ability to move "rhythmically and easily with each other"?

23. This description of community that Paul gives sounds nearly impossible—especially since we're talking about people! How would the fruit of the Spirit make such community tangible?

24. How do you think unbelievers would respond to a community like the one Paul describes?

Let's Act *(15 minutes)*
25. What steps will you take to help one another develop the fruit of the Spirit in each of your lives? (Remember, the fruit is produced by the Spirit, so be thinking about what role we play in its development.)

26. What are some steps you can take to become more like the community described in Ephesians 4?

GROUP WORSHIP   (15-30 minutes)

27. Design your own time of worship based on the information in this session. Ask the Holy Spirit to work within your group, creating the kind of community that God desires for you to share. Pray for ways to develop the fruit of the new life you have in God, and ask for guidance as you relate with one another.

Let's Listen to God *(15 minutes)*
28. After reading aloud the three commitments on pages 40-41, discuss what you sense the Holy Spirit is communicating to your group about your relationships with each other. Then take a moment to close your conversation in prayer.

7.
BRINGING COMMUNITY TO THE WORLD

"Peace I leave with you; my peace I give you. I do not give to you as the world gives. Do not let your hearts be troubled and do not be afraid."

—*John 14:27*

OVERVIEW

The kind of community for which God has designed us is unlike anything the world can offer. The community of believers is designed to accept people as they are, provide for each other's needs, love one another wholeheartedly, forgive wrongs, use conflict to grow, receive supernatural guidance, and more. But not all believers experience the kind of community God planned for us.

In this session we will review what it means to be a community that honors God. We will examine the purpose of community and explore ways to spread that community to believers outside this group and to the world itself. Your goal is to understand the purpose of community and discover ways to share that community with others.

So, what's the big deal?

The ideal community that God designed for us is rare—nothing in the world comes even close. How can we spread this kind of community to others and draw them into the body of Christ?

1. What are some of the groups (reading groups, PTA, classes, sports teams, et cetera) to which you belong?

2. How are those groups different from the group with whom you are studying this guide?

IN OTHER GROUPS	IN THIS GROUP

3. Think about the relationships you've formed in these groups. Again, how are they different?

IN OTHER GROUPS	IN THIS GROUP

4. How would you sum up the differences?

One of the things that makes a community of believers different from other kinds of groups is its purpose. Not only did God design us to be in relationship, He designed those relationships to help us grow and to change us to be more like Jesus Christ.

The writer of Hebrews recognized the importance of community—especially when life gets busy.

> And let us consider how we may spur one another on toward love and good deeds. Let us not give up meeting together, as some are in the habit of doing, but let us encourage one another—and all the more as you see the Day approaching. (Hebrews 10:24-25)

5. What does this passage say we are to do?

6. Why do you think it's so important to meet together?

7. What are some of the reasons we often "give up meeting together"?

8. How has encouragement helped you grow in the past?

In Galatians, the apostle Paul gives more reasons why community is vital to our growth in Christ.

> If someone is caught in a sin, you who are spiritual should restore him gently. But watch yourself, or you also may be tempted. Carry each other's burdens, and in this way you will fulfill the law of Christ. (Galatians 6:1-2)

9. What does Paul say we should do when others sin? Why?

10. How does being confronted with sin make you grow?

11. What is the law of Christ (see Matthew 22:35-40)?

12. How does carrying each other's burdens fulfill this law?

13. What would it look like to carry the burdens of others in your group?

For Further Study

Most communities have rules that members are expected to follow. The community of believers is no different. Throughout the New Testament we find specific rules or commands for how we are to treat other members. Use a concordance or Bible software program to look up the "one anothers"—the code of conduct for a Christian community.

 GROUP DISCOVERY (50-90 minutes)

Let's Warm Up (10 minutes)

14. What are some of the things that you need from other people to be most effective as a servant of Christ?

Let's Talk (30-50 minutes)

15. Discuss the "On Your Own" questions. What did you learn about the purpose of community?

16. In session 2 you came up with a group definition for "community." Go back to that now. Has your definition of community changed during the past weeks? If so, how?

17. Revise your definition of community to include any new ideas or experiences you've shared as a group.

The community we are to share as believers is different from any other community found in the world. Part of that difference is the faith we share. Jesus described His life in us as a light. Have someone read the following passage out loud.

> You are the light of the world. A city on a hill cannot be hidden. Neither do people light a lamp and put it under a bowl. Instead they put it on its stand, and it gives light to everyone in the house. In the same way, let your light shine before men, that they may see your good deeds and praise your Father in heaven. (Matthew 5:14-16)

18. Why do you think Jesus compared believers to light?

19. Why can't light be hidden?

20. How is your group like a light?

21. What are some of the ways that your group shines to others? (If you can't think of any ways, why do you think that's the case?)

Jesus gave the Great Commission to instruct the disciples about what they were to do with the gospel, the "good news," after Jesus returned to the Father.

Then Jesus came to them and said, "All authority in heaven and on earth has been given to me. Therefore go and make disciples of all nations, baptizing them in the name of the Father and of the Son and of the Holy Spirit, and teaching them to obey everything I have commanded you. And surely I am with you always, to the very end of the age." (Matthew 28:18-20)

22. Sometimes it can be frustrating to share the gospel with others. They don't see it as "good news"—they are distracted by the hypocrisy and division they see in the church, and by their fear of rules and regulations. How does community affect the way the gospel is perceived and received by others?

23. Who are some people you know who need the support of a group like yours but may not realize their need for God?

24. How can your community become a stepping stone for the gospel in their lives?

25. What are some things you can do as a community to let your light shine more brightly?

Let's Act (15 minutes)

26. Take some time to share specific things about:

a. What this community has meant to you

b. How God has used this group to bring you closer to Himself

c. What you appreciate about the others in this group

GROUP WORSHIP **(15-30 minutes)**

27. Design your own time of worship based on the material in this session. If your group is so inclined, sing an appropriate hymn or chorus. Then, divide into smaller groups of two or three for prayer. Some sample prayers about community based on passages from *The Message* are printed below.

Father, I ask You to strengthen us by Your Spirit—not a brute strength but a glorious inner strength—that Christ will live in us as we open the door and invite Him in. And I ask You that with both feet planted firmly on love, we'll be able to take in with each other and with all believers the extravagant dimensions of Christ's love. Help us to reach out and experience its breadth. To test its length. To plumb its depths. To rise to its heights. To live full lives, full in the fullness of You, our God. (from Ephesians 3)

Father, Help us to run on the road that You've called us to

travel. Help us to do this with humility and discipline—not in fits and starts, but steadily, pouring ourselves out for each other in acts of love, alert at noticing differences and quick at mending fences.

We were called to travel together on the same road and in the same direction. Help us to stay together, both outwardly and inwardly. You are our one Master; we have one faith, one baptism, one God and Father of all. You rule over all, work through all, and are present in all. Help everything we are and think and do to be permeated with Your Oneness. (from Ephesians 4)

Father, We pray that you will fill us with the knowledge of Your will through all spiritual wisdom and understanding. We pray this so that we may live lives worthy of You and that please You in every way: that we may bear fruit in every good work, that we may grow in our knowledge of You, that we may be strengthened with all power according to Your glorious might. Give us great endurance and patience. Help us to joyfully give You thanks for redeeming us and qualifying us to share in the inheritance of the saints in Your kingdom of light. We praise You for rescuing us from the dominion of darkness and for bringing us into the kingdom of Your Son, whom You love and in whom we have the forgiveness of sins. (from Colossians 1)

Let's Listen to God (15 minutes)

28. After reading aloud the three commitments on pages 40-41, discuss what you sense the Holy Spirit is communicating to your group about the following areas. Then close in prayer.

☐ Your worship and relationship with God

☐ Your relationships with each other

☐ Your relationships with those outside this group

8.
LET'S PERSONALIZE RELATIONSHIPS

OVERVIEW

In this session and the next, you will review and apply the lessons you have learned in sessions 2–7. In this session you will focus on personal lessons and applications, while session 9 will focus on group applications. As you prepare for your group meeting, remember to pray frequently. Some inventory work will help you select the one key truth from sessions 2–7 that is most urgent for you personally. Then your group will help you think through appropriate action steps and life changes you can pursue. Your goal will be to settle on one key truth and the action you can take to build it into your life.

So what's the big deal?
It's better to be obedient in just one area about which God is convicting you than to fill up a workbook full of good intentions about several truths, none of which you obey or profit from.

ON YOUR OWN   (30-60 minutes)

1. What changes are you beginning to see in your relationship with God as a result of this study?

☐ Any mistakes you are avoiding?

☐ Any attitudes you are changing?

☐ Any areas of new freedom in Christ?

☐ Any changes in the way you view God?

☐ Any new ways you feel or things you do when you spend time with God?

2. Review what you have studied and discussed in sessions 2 through 7. Try to state one or two truths that stand out to you as most important in each session. For example, you might write for session 7, "The quality of my relationships with other believers will directly and profoundly affect my ability to draw others to Christ."

☐ Session 2

☐ Session 3

☐ Session 4

☐ Session 5

☐ Session 6

☐ Session 7

3. You may have repeated yourself in question 2, circling around the same one or two truths that jump out at you from every session. If so, it may be that the Holy Spirit has put His finger on an area of focus. Take a moment to pray about your list of truths. Put a star beside the one that you think is most important for you to address in the near future. Or, combine several of the truths into one, and state it below. (Don't get sidetracked trying to summarize all of your truths into one overarching thesis. The point is to pick one limited idea that you can reasonably grasp and focus on.)

4. How has this truth affected your thinking and behavior so far?

5. How do you think the Holy Spirit would like this truth to affect your life—your thoughts, feelings, and actions?

Be prepared to share your key truth and its effects with your group. They will help you formulate a plan for integrating that truth into your life and acting on it. They will also help keep you accountable to the degree that you allow them to do so. You're not in this alone!

 GROUP DISCOVERY (50-90 minutes)

Let's Warm Up (10 minutes)
6. What is one thing you have gained from this group during the past seven sessions? What is one thing for which you are grateful?

Let's Talk (45-80 minutes)
Plan your time so that you have at least five minutes for each person to share his or her truth and receive help in formulating a plan of action. Ten minutes each would be even better, but that might require going overtime. Be sure that no one is shortchanged of this opportunity for help.

7. Read to your group your key truth, how it has affected you so far, and how you think the Spirit would like it to affect you. Then, with help from the group, come up with a plan for integrating your key truth into your life. Ask yourselves the following questions as you help each other plan your strategies:

☐ Is the key truth clear?
☐ What results or outcomes would you like to see from this plan of action?
☐ Are the action steps specific and realistic?
☐ Not all action steps in the spiritual realm are quantifiable. For example, praying for thirty minutes a day is quantifiable, but genuinely opening your heart to God in prayer is not. How will you know if the changes you are pursuing are really happening?

Here is an example of a plan that is practical, specific, measurable, and clear:

I think that, for me, the number one barrier to relationships is my tendency to hold on to wrongs done against me. I expect others to earn their way back into my good graces. I am going to memorize Matthew 6:14-15 and recite it to myself each morning. Each evening before I go to bed, I'm going to review the day and see when I have had a forgiving spirit toward others, and when I have "kept a record of wrongs." Then I'll decide if I need to speak to the person about the matter, or just let it go. One person in this group will check with me by phone every couple of days for the next month to see how I'm doing on developing this quality of forgiveness.

Write your plan here (you may continue on the top of the next page):

8. List anything you have committed to do for someone else in your group:

9. Use this space to list the other group members' key truths (you will need these to do your personal preparation for session 9):

GROUP WORSHIP (15-30 minutes)

10. Design and implement your own time of worship. Be sure to include prayer about your key truth and your plans for applying it.

9.
LET'S GROW TOGETHER THROUGH RELATIONSHIPS

OVERVIEW

The work you do this session will be similar to session 8 in that you will review and apply the lessons you have learned in sessions 2–7. In this session your goal is to come up with an application for your whole group, whereas last time the focus was on personal application.

Planning group applications requires hard work. You will be thinking in areas that may be different from anything you have tried before. Six areas have been selected to help you evaluate your group's progress.

So what's the big deal?
If you persevere, you will achieve powerful results. You will be growing not just as individuals but also as a community of believers.

ON YOUR OWN   (30-60 minutes)

Throughout the course of these studies, you have had experiences that contributed to your sense of community. Take a few minutes to assess the progress and contributions your group has made in spiritual sensitivity, worship dynamics, relational intimacy, functional interdependence, mission focus, and sphere of influence. This assessment procedure will help you evaluate your group's progress and help you plan for your future relationships.

1. **Ability to listen to the Holy Spirit.** In a group with high sensitivity to the Spirit, you will observe unity and peace created by the Spirit, or you will observe people allowing the Spirit to disrupt their complacency and challenge their assumptions. On a scale of 1 (low) to 5 (high), how would you rate your group's sensitivity, receptivity, and responsiveness to the Holy Spirit's leadership?

1	2	3	4	5
low				high

2. **Worship dynamics.** God is the central focus in worship. Recall your worship times in the preceding sessions. In a group with "rich" worship dynamics you can expect to find a sense of God's majestic presence with you, variety, and everyone participating and contributing. On a scale of 1 (poor) to 5 (rich), how would you assess the overall quality of your group's worship experience?

1	2	3	4	5
poor				rich

3. **Relational intimacy.** The Bible is full of relational terms such as love, forgiveness, acceptance, reconciliation, and bearing one another's burdens. As you experience these conditions, your group will grow in relational intimacy. Evidences of "deep" intimacy are high levels of trust, vulnerability, transparency, honesty, and mutual commitment. On a scale of 1 (shallow) to 5 (deep), how would you assess your group's level of intimacy?

1	2	3	4	5
shallow				deep

4. **Functional interdependence.** The church is the body of Christ, a living organism with many members. Your small group functions like a system in that body, working interdependently with other systems and their members. Not only that, each member of your group is gifted to perform specific tasks that contribute to the overall internal functions of your group. On a scale of 1 (harsh, grating) to 5 (sweet, synchronized), how well are the members of

your community working together toward a common task, and
how harmoniously is your community working alongside others?

1	2	3	4	5
harsh, grating				sweet, synchronized

5. **Mission focus.** Christian communities can easily become self-absorbed. This happens when they turn a deaf ear or a blind eye to what's on God's heart and, instead, focus their attention on themselves. The result is a diminished heart for the world that God loves and gave His Son to die for. God uses groups to reach into every nook and cranny of the world. On a scale of 1 (self-absorbed) to 5 (other-focused), how motivated is your group to looking beyond itself and fulfilling God's mission to reach the world?

1	2	3	4	5
self-absorbed				other-focused

6. **Sphere of influence.** God's mission is global in scope, including all kinds of people—rich and poor, men and women, young and old, Black, White, Hispanic, Asian, et cetera. Although we are to be open to new ministry opportunities, God often calls a community to minister within its specific sphere of influence. This sphere sets limits that sharpen your focus. On a scale of 1 (confused, non-existent) to 5 (sharply focused), how clear is it to your community whom God has called you to minister to?

1	2	3	4	5
confused				focused

7. Review all the truths and life applications that you and your fellow group members identified last time. What is the one truth from these studies that you feel is most relevant for your whole group collectively? (This may be different from what is most significant to you personally.)

GROUP DISCOVERY   (50-90 minutes)

Let's Warm Up (10 minutes)

8. What is one way this group has helped you grow in the way you handle relationships?

Let's Talk (30-45 minutes)

9. Share progress on personal applications from the last session. Are you helping each other follow through on your commitments? How so? Thank God for the progress He has already made among you.

10. Remember, community building is a process. Some members of your group may desire greater intimacy, and some may feel threatened by the intimacy already achieved. God is still at work in your group in the six areas you assessed on pages 90-91. He is molding you into a vehicle fit for Him to use however He wills. Review the six areas of assessment and compare answers as a group. Pay special attention to major differences in your evaluations. How do you account for these differences?

11. Discuss what each of you thinks is the one significant truth most relevant to your group (identified in question 7). Try to come to a group consensus of the one truth and its implications for your group. To reach that consensus, here are some helpful hints:
    ☐ Begin with prayer, asking God to clarify your thinking.
    ☐ List the truth from each individual on a chart or white board.
    ☐ Look for duplications and related themes. Consolidate and combine where possible.

- ☐ Build consensus on one truth. Sometimes related thoughts can be combined to better reflect the overall truth but beware of stringing ideas together into a broad, complicated conglomeration.
- ☐ Don't worry about a perfect statement. Blend the ideas of each person in the group to arrive at the consensus position. (Designate someone in the group who has an aptitude with words to edit for clarity and length. Take the statement home to polish it up, if necessary.)

12. Write your group truth here.

13. Next you will plan how to integrate this truth into your group life, much as you did for each individual group member last time. Your first step will be prayer. Take five minutes to ask God to lead you in this process. You might ask, "Lord, how would you like our group to put this truth into practice?" or "God, what would you like our community to become?" Listen quietly. As you have thoughts or impressions, either make mental notes or jot them down.

14. Write three headings on newsprint or a white board: God, One Another, Others. Under the first heading, list ways in which this truth should affect your group's relationship with God. Under the second heading, list ways in which this truth should affect your relationships with each other, and so on.

God	One Another	Others

15. Now brainstorm a fourth list: things you can do to put this truth into practice in your group. Call out ideas without evaluating or criticizing any of them.

16. After five or ten minutes, stop and sort the ideas into short-range steps and long-range steps. Edit them so that each one is a realistic, doable action that lends itself to accountability. Who will do what, by when, where, and for/with whom? Weed out any impractical ideas. Try to come up with at least one short-range and one long-range step that meet these standards.
    ☐ What is it?
    ☐ Who will do what?
    ☐ By when?
    ☐ Where?
    ☐ For/with whom?

    a. Short-range steps

    b. Long-range steps

Because learning to implement this truth as a community is so important, you should commit yourselves to take as many sessions as needed to work out your group application. Place a higher priority on implementing your plan rather than moving on to another study.

GROUP WORSHIP (15-30 minutes)

17. Design and implement your own time of worship. Be sure to include prayer about your key truth and your plans for applying it. Also, thank God for what you have received from this study. Celebrate your time together, both your past and your future.

If you set out to identify the core elements of the Christian life, what would your list include?

After ten years of Bible study involving thousands of believers from countries all around the world, The Navigators' SCRIPTURAL ROOTS OF LIFE team saw a few basic themes emerge over and over again:

WORSHIP
Worship: Honoring God in All of Life
(ISBN: 1-57683-007-1; 9 sessions; 96 pages)

COMMUNITY
Relationships: Resolving Conflict and Building Community
(ISBN: 1-57683-023-3; 9 sessions; 96 pages)

INTIMACY WITH GOD
Intimacy: Pursuing Intimacy with God
(ISBN: 1-57683-010-1; 9 sessions; 96 pages)

BECOMING LIKE CHRIST
Christlikeness: Committing Ourselves to be Changed by God
(ISBN: 1-57683-006-3; 9 sessions; 96 pages)

THE TRINITY
Restoration: Discovering How God Meets Our Deepest Needs
(ISBN: 1-57683-009-8; 9 sessions; 96 pages)

THE UNSEEN WORLD
Warfare: Discovering the Reality of the Unseen World
(ISBN: 1-57683-026-8; 9 sessions; 96 pages)

SHARING THE FAITH
Outreach: Sharing the Real Gospel with the World
(ISBN: 1-57683-012-8; 9 sessions; 96 pages)

WORK
Work: Serving God on the Job
(ISBN: 1-57683-024-1; 9 sessions; 96 pages)

Designed to foster close-knit community within your group, the FOUNDATIONS FOR CHRISTIAN LIVING series is a great way to grow strong in faith, life, and love for God. Available at your local Christian bookstore. Or call 1-800-366-7788 to order.

NAVPRESS
BRINGING TRUTH TO LIFE